Introducing
BUDDHISM

VADANYA
(Chris Pauling)

**BARNES
& NOBLE
BOOKS**

NEW YORK

2001 Barnes & Noble Books

ISBN 0-7607-2674-4

Printed and bound in the United States of America

05 06 MC 9 8 7 6 5 4

QWV

CONTENTS

One

WHAT *IS* BUDDHISM?

BUDDHISM IS PROBABLY the fastest growing spiritual tradition in the Western world. At a time when we seem to be presented with a choice between a narrow, materialistic world view that offers little meaning in life, and traditional religions that make too many demands on our credulity for many of us to accept, Buddhism offers a very old – but very radical – alternative. More and more people are coming to realize that in rejecting the religious beliefs traditional in our society we have thrown the spiritual baby out with the unreasonable bathwater, and are turning to Buddhism as a way of rediscovering the human and spiritual values so lacking in the bleak consumerism of our times.

Yet for many people Buddhism is a puzzling phenomenon, and reading a few books on the subject often does little to clear up the confusion. It is not that the teachings of Buddhism are particularly hard to grasp. Rather the very nature of Buddhism seems to lie outside the categories in which we Westerners are used to thinking, so that we find it difficult to get a clear picture of what it is all about. Because of this – and despite the enormous amount said and written on the subject – most Westerners still have no clear idea what Buddhism really is.

Some authors talk of Buddhism as a religion like other religions. Others see it mainly as a philosophy, in the sense of a reasonable, thought-out approach to existence, even portraying it as something rather intellectual and coldly rational. Yet others seem to regard it mainly as a therapy, presenting Buddhist meditation as a cure for the damage done to us by the neurotic society in which we live. But Buddhism does not fit very comfortably into any one of these pigeon-holes.

Certainly if we look it up in an encyclopedia we will find Buddhism classed as one of the world's great religions, alongside Christianity, Judaism, and Islam. But Buddhism is very different from our usual idea of a religion, in several important ways. It has no God we must obey. It has no dogma we must believe in. And it does not ask us to give up our freedom and individuality to any higher authority, but instead encourages us to stand up proudly and take responsibility for our own vision of what it means to be a human being.

But if Buddhism is not exactly what we normally think of as a religion, it is much more than just a philosophy. The tools of philosophy are words, logic, and reason. Buddhism aims to open our being to truths that go beyond the realm of reason, truths which are grasped as much by our emotions and intuition as by our intellect.

Again some people see Buddhism, and Buddhist meditation techniques in particular, as another entry in the long menu of therapies currently on offer. Certainly Buddhism does provide us with practical, effective ways to change old and unhelpful habits of thought and behaviour, to become happier, healthier, and more potent human beings. But it is not just another therapy: it aims not only to make sick people well, but also to make well people much more than merely healthy. The aim of Buddhist meditation is not only to resolve psychological problems, but also to open doors to states of consciousness that are beyond the imagination of Western psychology. Buddhism offers a spiritual and transcendental perspective, and its vision of what a human being can become takes us far beyond the province of psychology.

Perhaps it is best not to try to imprison Buddhism in our preconceived categories. After all the very word 'Buddhism' is a Western invention. Eastern Buddhists do not normally talk of 'Buddhism' at all: they speak simply of the 'Buddha-Dhamma', or 'Dharma'. Dharma is a Sanskrit word which means both the truth itself and any teaching that helps us to realize this truth in our lives and in ourselves. To the Buddhist the Dharma is nothing less than a blueprint for the unfolding of the full potential of human consciousness, a clearly laid-out path of development by means of which we can grow beyond our accidental conditioning and wake up to the true nature of reality.

Some 2,500 years ago the founder of Buddhism stated that any teaching that genuinely helps people to develop should be considered to be Dharma. His followers took him at his word, and in the many centuries since the Buddha's death they have evolved a wide range of 'skilful means' to help human beings outgrow their self-imposed limitations, all clearly derived from the Buddha's original teachings, but all adapted to the particular needs of different times, places, cultures, and temperaments. To get at the common essence that underlies these diverse cultural forms of Buddhism we need first of all to consider the Buddha himself and the nature of his achievement, then to examine the main elements of his teachings, and thirdly to discuss some of the principal ways in which these teachings have found expression in the lives of his followers over the last two and a half millennia.

Two

THE BUDDHA

'Buddha' is a Sanskrit word meaning 'One who is awake'.
The founder of Buddhism was not a god, a prophet, or a
messiah. He was a normal human being who, by his own
efforts, became completely awake, both to his own potential
and to the nature of the world around him. This state of
being fully awake – usually called 'Enlightenment' – is what
Buddhism is all about. Since the Buddha's time many other
men and women have also achieved this state of Enlightenment, but the title 'Buddha' is usually reserved for the
trailblazer, the man who discovered the path to Enlightenment and erected the signposts for others to follow.

Siddhartha Gautama – the man who became this trailblazer – was born into a prosperous aristocratic family of the
Shakya clan of Nepal and northern India some time around
560BCE.* Some traditions say that his father was king of the
Shakyas, and although this may not be historically accurate,

---

* Buddhists and other non-Christians do not use the abbreviations
AD – 'Year of our Lord' – and BC. They refer to years under this
accepted dating convention as either CE (Common Era) or BCE
(before Common Era).

it seems certain that as a child and young adult Siddhartha lived a very opulent life. We can imagine an existence of undisguised luxury, with exquisite food, gorgeous clothing, and many servants, lived out against the backdrop of a sub-Himalayan India which at that time must have been close to being an earthly paradise.

But despite all this he was not happy. The pleasures that surrounded him on every side could not drown out a deeper sense of dissatisfaction, a deeper desire for meaning. This may strike a chord with many people today in the West, where material needs are satisfied relatively easily, and where the opportunities for leisure and amusement would be the envy of previous generations. Yet a glance at the faces of the passers-by in any Western city will show that this prosperity does not necessarily bring happiness. Like Siddhartha many of us find a life devoted to material pleasure to be empty and unfulfilling.

Siddhartha's dissatisfaction with his luxurious existence reached a head when he was twenty-nine years old, when he made the decision to leave his family home and his life of luxury, and to become a wandering seeker after truth, his only possessions a begging-bowl and a simple robe.

The world into which Siddhartha launched himself was technologically primitive by our standards, but philosophically it was very rich – far more so than the modern West. The early Buddhist scriptures give the impression of a society with a deep interest in the fundamental questions of existence. Competing meditation teachers and philosophical schools were rife, and religious debate was a popular pastime.

In this atmosphere Siddhartha spent six years wandering, meditating, and learning what he could from the teachers he met, strenuously determined to find what had been lacking in his pampered life at home. For a while he even devoted himself to extreme asceticism, going without food and sleep in the hope that this would help him to realize the truth. He then realized that denying the body was not a useful spiritual practice and, turning his back on ascetic practice, devoted himself wholeheartedly to meditation.

At the end of his six years of determined effort, on the night of the first full moon of the month Vesakha in the year 528BCE, Siddhartha Gautama sat down to meditate under a pipal tree on the banks of the River Niranjana, at the site which later came to be known as Bodh Gaya, vowing not to get up until he had found what he was looking for. By now his determination had become unstoppable. He entered a state of deep meditation, and as the night wore on his awareness penetrated layer after layer of the nature of reality, until he achieved a total and direct perception of the truth. By the time he saw the morning star rise over the eastern horizon he knew that his liberation was unshakeable. Siddhartha Gautama had become the Buddha, the Awakened One.

The entire Buddhist tradition exists to help others experience this same awakening and liberation for themselves, and later we will have much more to say both about the nature of the Buddha's Enlightenment, and about the practical means that Buddhists use to help them follow in his footsteps. But first we will describe the rest of the Buddha's life, and the extraordinary effects his awakening produced in the society he was born into – effects which are still echoing around the world 2,500 years after his death.

For several weeks after his Enlightenment the Buddha continued to meditate near the River Niranjana, digesting the full implications of his experience. At first he thought that he would never be able to communicate his realization – that nobody would or could understand what he was talking about – and he was tempted simply to pass the rest of his life enjoying the bliss of his liberation, leaving the rest of humanity to its own devices. But he quickly realized that the very nature of his awakening ruled out this sort of selfishness. His sense of unity with all living beings meant that he felt impelled to share his experience, no matter how impossible this seemed.

We are told that during this period he had a vision in which he saw humanity as a lake of lotus plants in bud. Some buds were still buried in the mud of the lake bottom. Others were growing up through the water, but were still muddy and tightly shut. A few buds had already reached the surface, and needed only a little prompting to allow them to open in the sunlight. This image of men and women as developing beings growing out of the mud and darkness towards the light gave him the encouragement he needed. Heartened by the fact that a few people might already be developed enough to receive his teachings, while others could be helped to grow until they reached this stage, he set out to communicate the incommunicable.

A week later he gave his first discourse in the Deer Park at Benares, about a hundred miles from Bodh Gaya. Here he came across a group of ascetics who had known him in earlier days, and who had been disgusted when he renounced asceticism. Now at first they refused to listen to him or even to greet him. But one by one they were convinced by the overwhelming force of the Buddha's words and being, and one by one they became his followers.

For the next forty-five years the Buddha spent nine months of every year walking the length and breadth of a vast tract of northern India spreading his teaching, and again and again this pattern would be repeated. Again and again he would talk to men and women from all classes and walks of life, singly, in groups of tens or even of hundreds, and again and again the power of his presence and his words helped them to see life with different eyes. Again and again they would express their commitment to living by the vision the Buddha had revealed to them, and would become his followers.

Of course not everyone who came into contact with the Buddha was convinced. But in an age with no telecommunications and primitive transport his teachings and personal influence spread through northern India at a remarkable rate. During his lifetime his following grew to such proportions that he was accused of disrupting society. By the time of his death at the age of eighty his teachings had exerted a profound social, cultural, and spiritual influence within seven nations covering an area of some 50,000 square miles. The rulers of the two major kingdoms of northern India and many other leading figures of the day were among his disciples. And he had established a 'sangha' or spiritual community drawn from both sexes and all castes and levels of society which is still thriving today. All this was achieved despite the fact that his teachings on social issues were often unpopular and subversive, in particular his criticism of the caste system and his outspoken comments on the religious pretensions of the hereditary priestly caste.

How do we explain the Buddha's phenomenal success in attracting followers and spreading his teaching, at a time when so many other spiritual teachers were competing to be heard? No doubt this achievement stems partly from the teachings themselves, which can still strike many people as being so obviously true they feel they must always have known them. But the Buddha's words on their own are probably not enough to explain his success – the nature of the man who was speaking the words played the decisive role. The Buddha was not just talking *about* Enlightenment or the way to achieve it. The Buddha *was himself* Enlightened, and – for anyone with eyes to see – his Enlightenment showed. He himself was walking, talking proof of the truth of his teachings which only the most stubborn witness could deny.

The picture of the Buddha we get from the earliest Buddhist writings is of a man of great dignity who towers above the circumstances in which he finds himself, a man of complete fearlessness and unshakeable self-confidence whose mental composure is quite unaffected even by pain, illness, and his own imminent death. At the same time this awe-inspiring figure is open and approachable, willing to devote his time to anyone regardless of class, education, or intelligence. We see a man of great compassion, a man without anger who treats conflict and stupidity with gentle, affectionate irony. In his dealings with pig-headedness or foolishness on the part of his followers we see the gentle, humorous touch of a man who has seen through to the core of reality, but who retains great warmth, sympathy, and respect for those who are still trapped in delusion.

Finally we see a leader who is regarded with awe and reverence, but has no desire to be followed blindly, and who now and then shows a hint of good-humoured exasperation at the unwillingness of some of his followers to think and act for themselves.

This picture, faded as it is by the passage of twenty-five centuries, gives us a glimpse of what the Buddha looked like *from the outside*. But to have any idea of the Buddha's real nature we need to consider not just how he appeared to an external observer in his day-to-day life. We need to consider his nature *from the inside* – to consider the nature of Enlightenment itself.

ENLIGHTENMENT

Enlightenment is the final goal of the Buddhist path, and anyone with an interest in Buddhism will obviously want to be told exactly what it is. Unfortunately this is impossible! To try to *describe* Enlightenment is like trying to describe the colour blue to someone who has been blind from birth – words simply are not up to the job. An often quoted analogy from the Zen tradition compares talking about Enlightenment to pointing a finger at the moon. The finger can point out where to look to see the moon, but it is not the moon itself – and if we end up staring at the finger we have made a serious mistake. Having said this we will try to point a very shaky finger at Enlightenment.

Enlightenment is a state of being, and because being has many different facets, Enlightenment too can be approached from several points of view.

Looked at from the point of view of wisdom, Enlightenment is direct insight into the nature of reality. It is a direct experience of the truth behind and beyond the world, and behind our part in it – which is something quite different from holding intellectual views about the nature of life and the universe. The effect of this aspect of Enlightenment is often described in quite negative terms, as an annihilation of the sense of self. But this transcendental insight does not so much annihilate our sense of self as expand it far beyond our normal narrow view. By stepping beyond the boundaries of any one small self the Enlightened being becomes something much larger, and sees the universe from the widest possible perspective. The whole of Buddhism can be seen as an attempt to persuade us to expand our vision of who and what we are, and so move towards the vast perspectives of Buddhahood.

Although we have used words like 'insight' and 'perspective', Enlightenment is as much about feeling as it is about knowing. Transcendental insight goes hand in hand with the deepest possible transformation of the emotions – it brings a sense of oneness with all other beings, and a huge, compassionate heart for all that lives.

Traditionally Enlightenment is sometimes spoken of as the 'Heart's Release' – for many people a much more evocative phrase than 'insight into reality', and one that brings home a little of these more emotional aspects. If from one point of view Buddhism can be seen as a way of gradually expanding the boundaries that define what we regard as 'ourselves', from another it can just as validly be seen as a way of allowing us gradually to open our heart. And each step towards a more positive and loving approach to life – each small opening of the heart – makes us happier and more fulfilled, and moves us a little closer to the final heart's release of Enlightenment.

We have talked about Enlightenment mainly in terms of wisdom and compassion. But it has also been described in several other ways: as a state of complete liberation and limitless energy; as the end of all our worries, all our sorrows, all our unhappiness; as the bliss of pure being.

It sounds marvellous. But does it really exist? If it does, and if we really can achieve it, we would surely be very foolish to run around after anything else. But how can we be sure?

On this as on all other points Buddhism does not ask for blind faith – a very un-Buddhist 'virtue'. Instead it encourages us to develop a reasoned confidence. We can develop a reasoned confidence that Enlightenment exists as a real possibility both because we see evidence of it in others, and because we have an intuition of the potential for Enlightenment in ourselves – an intuition which becomes progressively stronger as we take even our first faltering steps towards our own 'Heart's Release'.

Some Buddhists are lucky enough to have close contact with a teacher who is near enough to Enlightenment to provide living evidence of its existence, in the same way that the Buddha provided this evidence in his lifetime. But even at a lower level, as we become involved with people who have systematically worked on themselves over a period of years, we begin to meet people who, although they may not be fully Enlightened, are certainly closer to this state than we are. We also see that these people themselves keep growing, keep moving in the right direction. This gives us a firm confidence that real, significant spiritual growth *is* possible – and that if there are any limits to growth – which Buddhism denies – these occur somewhere very far beyond where most of us are at the moment.

But even without the evidence of other people, we have all seen at least a distant glimmer of the Enlightened state within ourselves. We all carry the potential for Enlightenment, in much the same way that an acorn carries the potential to be an oak tree. It is this seed that allows us to respond to the ideal, and which occasionally gives us a dim echo of Enlightenment in the best moments of our lives – those moments of beauty, love, or inspiration, when the small personal preoccupations that normally cast such dark shadows in our minds melt away like mist.

Not only do we all carry the seed of Enlightenment within us, we also have a natural urge to grow towards the liberated state, like the urge of a plant to grow towards the light. Most of the time this urge may be drowned out by the confusion of our everyday lives. But when we do respond to it we know instinctively that we are moving in the right direction. Every step we take towards Enlightenment brings a sense of expansion, and makes us feel happier, healthier, and more fulfilled. This is not abstract theorizing. It is a matter of direct personal experience for many people. The best way to develop confidence that Enlightenment exists is to take even a small step towards it, and see what happens.

Three

ETHICS

BUDDHISM IS A practical tradition. It does not just offer an inspiring vision of what a human being can become. It also provides a large number of effective techniques and practices to help us grow towards this ideal and make it a real force in our everyday lives.

But these techniques and practices are not meant to be used at random. To be effective they must be applied wisely and appropriately, taking into account the needs of the individual and the stage of development he or she has reached. Of course different people grow in different ways. But the dynamics of spiritual development can be seen to follow an overall pattern, and at least in its broad outlines this is the same for everyone.

Buddhism often uses the analogy of the path to describe this pattern, formulating the process of growth in terms of a sequence of stages the individual must pass through, one after the other, in order to reach the goal of Enlightenment. Over the centuries the Buddhist tradition has given rise to a number of different formulations of this path, all describing the same underlying process, but expressing it in different words, giving it different emphases, or chopping it up into different numbers of steps.

An account of even a few of these formulations is beyond the scope of a short book, so we will concentrate only on the simplest and most general: the threefold division of the path into the aspects of Ethics, Meditation, and Wisdom. We will describe each of these aspects in more detail in the following sections, but first there are two general points that need to be made.

The first is that the analogy of the path should not be taken too strictly. We do not have to finish one stage before we can begin the next. Although meditation follows ethics in the sequence this does not mean that there is no point in taking up meditation until our ethics are perfect. In this sense spiritual development is less like a path than like the unfolding of the petals of a flower, in which all the petals unfold together, but none can unfold faster than the previous one allows. Hence we may be able to get great benefits from meditation while still living what is in some ways an unethical life. But only up to a point. Sooner or later we will reach a stage where our meditation can go no further until we turn our attention to the ethical basis of our life.

The second general point is that we should not see the earlier stages of this path as unpleasant preliminaries that we endure with gritted teeth for the sake of our future happiness. If we are following the path in the right spirit we do not have to wait until we reach the goal of Enlightenment before we begin to see benefits. Each step should be accompanied by a feeling of expansion, a feeling that our life has become more meaningful, a feeling of being more creative and less the passive victim of events. If we do not experience such feelings we are probably doing something wrong.

Like every other aspect of Buddhist practice, Buddhist ethics are a means to an end – the end being Enlightenment. The closer we get to Enlightenment, the more irrelevant conscious ethical observances become, because we will begin to act quite naturally in a way that contributes to our own welfare and to the welfare of the world. But until that time we need to adopt certain ethical principles as a conscious practice. This does not mean that we must formalistically follow any set of rules. According to Buddhism it is the *state of mind* behind our actions that is important, and the practice of ethics is the way we work on our states of mind, not just while sitting on our meditation cushion, but in the all-important arena of everyday life.

This Buddhist idea of ethics is very different from our normal Western view. Many Westerners are used to thinking that to be ethical is to follow a list of regulations handed down by some higher authority, whether this be our parents, society, or God. Buddhist ethics on the other hand asks us to stand up and actively decide what sort of being we wish to be – and an essential part of doing this is to decide upon a moral code and honestly to try to live by it. To decide to be a Buddhist is to decide that, in whatever way our circumstances allow, the ideal of growing towards Enlightenment will take the highest priority in our lives, and we therefore need to live a life that helps rather than hinders our progress, and which expresses our ideals.

Buddhist ethics are about organizing our life so that positive emotions are encouraged, and so that negative emotions are calmed. They are about liberating ourselves from the slavery of unhelpful habits and conditioning, and becoming effective, potent individuals with control over the direction of our own lives. And they are about acting in a way that gives us a sense of wholeness and pride in honestly trying to live up to our vision of what we can become.

To be ethical in the Buddhist sense is to act intelligently in our own self-interest. But this does not mean that we should concentrate solely on ourselves. We cannot separate ourselves from others or the world around us. We are all part of each other: when we hurt another we also hurt ourselves, and when we benefit others we also benefit ourselves. Ultimately Buddhist ethics are about cultivating and expressing self-transcending wisdom in our daily lives, which means rising above our small personal point of view, and acting from an altogether more spacious, less self-centred perspective. This is to act in the best interests of our *real* selves, and also of other beings and the universe as a whole.

In the absence of a judging God the words 'right' and 'wrong' are inappropriate to the Buddhist idea of ethics. Instead Buddhism classes actions as either 'skilful' or 'unskilful'. Skilful behaviour is just what the word implies: it is intelligent behaviour, in that it contributes to our own happiness and to the happiness of others, in that it springs from and gives rise to positive, healthy states of mind, and in that it helps us to grow. Unskilful behaviour has the opposite effects, but usually it comes about because we do not see reality as it is, rather than because there is anything 'bad' about us as human beings.

Clearly ethics in this sense is a much wider issue than following a set of rules: it could include such considerations as where we live, who we choose to associate with, our job, our sexual relationships, our friendships, the food we eat, the books we read, what we choose to do with our leisure, and every other aspect of the way we order our life.

But although ethics is not really a matter of rules, Buddhism does provide a few simple guidelines. These 'precepts' (as these guidelines are called) are not commandments – in a tradition with no God the concept of a commandment is meaningless. They are rough benchmarks indicating how an Enlightened being would behave. Buddhists undertake to adopt these precepts as training principles, on the grounds that to consciously choose to behave like an Enlightened being allows us to become more like an Enlightened being. To fail to keep a precept is not a 'sin' – the concept does not exist in Buddhism – it is to fall below the standards we have set ourselves. And the emotional response to occasionally failing to live up to these standards should be quite different from the sense of guilt provoked by 'sinning' against more authoritarian systems of ethics.

Unfortunately many Westerners are burdened by feelings of irrational guilt, a legacy of religious attitudes which imagine God as a cosmic, judgemental authority figure who regards our normal biological drives as 'evil'. These attitudes – enshrined in the Christian dogma of 'original sin' – can lead to a deep-rooted sense of basic unworthiness. Such a negative view of oneself – and by implication of other people as well – makes it difficult to take a healthy attitude to ethics, which should encourage an open, happy, tolerant, and loving approach to life. Many of us need to defuse these feelings of irrational guilt – perhaps even by flouting *all* authority for a while, even that of 'God' – before we can undertake the Buddhist precepts in the right spirit. Probably all Westerners need to take care that they do not contaminate their attitude to the precepts by importing concepts like obedience and sin from other traditions.

But of course the fact that many people suffer from highly undesirable feelings of irrational guilt does not mean that guilt can never be rational – or even desirable. It can be reasonable, and indeed useful, to feel a sense of sorrow, disappointment, or remorse about failing to keep to the precepts in ways that harm ourselves or other beings, especially if these feelings lead us to break out of damaging habits or act more intelligently in future. But even when feelings of remorse *are* justified we should try to deal with them as quickly as possible, never letting them drag on when they are no longer useful, and never letting them damage our fundamental sense of self-worth.

The Buddhist precepts are traditionally couched in negative terms, as acts we undertake *not* to do. But each embodies a positive principle, a state of mind, or an emotion that we need to develop and express as part of our spiritual practice. It is these positive emotions and states of mind behind the precepts which are important. To abide by the letter of a precept without working on the positive principle that underlies it is as good as useless. But by working on the positive principles, with time the harmful actions that the negative forms of the precepts warn us against simply lose their appeal, and we can often grow beyond them quite painlessly, in much the same way that we have already grown out of the things that amused us in our childhood.

The exact form of the precepts differs a little between traditions, and also according to the level of commitment and development of the individual concerned. However, there are five ethical guidelines on which all Buddhists agree. These are explained, along with the positive principles underlying them in the next five sections.

TO REFRAIN FROM CAUSING HARM TO OTHER LIVING BEINGS

The positive principle underlying this precept is that we should try as far as possible to behave with friendliness, understanding, and loving-kindness towards ourselves, other people, animals, and even plants and the planet we live on. We have already seen that Enlightenment is as much about 'heart's release' as it is about wisdom – the two are inseparable – and the development of a warm, open heart is central to any sort of spiritual growth. Buddhists use a number of meditation practices to cultivate feelings of friendliness and compassion, but warm feelings on their own are not enough. These have to find expression in real acts of kindness.

The application of this precept begins with ourselves, then spreads outwards like ripples on a pond. It begins with ourselves because if we ourselves are unhappy we cannot begin to befriend others in any meaningful way, and much of our unhappiness is self-inflicted. To become happy we need to learn to love ourselves, and to be kind to ourselves – by dropping self-destructive habits, by getting rid of irrational guilts and anxieties, and by not allowing ourselves to become so hurried and stressed that we have no space to experience enjoyable states of mind.

But the positive principle behind the precept does not stop there. It also asks us to inject more loving-kindness into our relationships with those around us, starting with our immediate family and friends. It asks us to try to see these people as three-dimensional human beings, with their own needs and fears which are just as strong and valid as ours. And it asks us to show our friendliness and consideration for these people by real acts of kindness – by going out of our way to help them when they need help, by giving them presents even when it is not their birthday, by washing the dishes, by telling them how we feel about them. If we make a conscious effort to develop our friendships in this way, we quite quickly find that this has a dramatic effect on the quality of our relationships, and through these on our own lives and the lives of those around us.

Having become a friend to ourselves and to those closest to us, Buddhism then asks us to go even further: it asks us to become a friend to the whole world. Our warm feelings should extend not only to people we know but to people we have never seen. They should extend beyond humankind to all the other creatures that share our planet. And wherever possible we should make these feelings concrete by real acts of kindness. This Buddhist ideal of being a friend to the world finds its strongest expression in the ideal of the *bodhisattva* – Sanskrit for a being whose essence is Enlightenment. More will be said about the bodhisattva ideal in a later chapter, but very briefly a bodhisattva is someone who chooses to work selflessly for others on the basis of a profound experience of the unity of all conscious beings.

In its negative form – as something we undertake *not* to do rather than as a positive attitude we try to develop – this precept has a number of concrete implications. At its simplest level it asks us wherever possible to refrain from violence or other actions that would physically hurt living beings. It also asks us to refrain from harming beings in a mental or spiritual way – for example by causing mental anguish – and not to allow ourselves to become an accomplice in activities which cause harm or suffering to others.

Many Buddhists take this to imply that they should be vegetarian. Today in the West this seems particularly important in view of modern factory-farming methods, under which animals are caused a great deal of suffering just to provide us with a pleasant taste sensation at minimum cost. Some Western Buddhists take this precept to imply that they should not eat any animal products whatsoever, on the grounds that to consume eggs or dairy products involves acting as an accomplice in a cruel system of animal exploitation.

The precept also has implications for the way we earn our living. Obviously it would rule out work in the armed forces, the armaments industry, butchery and the meat trade, or any other industry that promotes violence and causes death or suffering, or that exploits people or other living beings for economic ends. At a more subtle level it might also raise doubts about forms of work that cause less obvious suffering, or cause harm on a more spiritual level – for example by promoting useless craving, as might be the case with work in the advertising industry, or in industries that produce unnecessary luxury goods. On the principle that the precept begins with ourselves it should also warn us against work that hinders our happiness or harms our growth, for example by subjecting us to so much hurry and stress that we find peace of mind impossible to attain.

TO REFRAIN FROM TAKING ANYTHING WHICH IS NOT FREELY GIVEN

The positive principle underlying this precept is that instead of taking from others we should try to be as generous and open-handed as possible, as a way of expressing our warm feelings and expanding our awareness beyond our own wants. Generosity has been described as the fundamental Buddhist virtue, because giving is an excellent way of overcoming our tight, painful obsession with our own little selves – which could be said to be what Buddhism is all about.

Generosity is an attitude of mind, but it is an attitude that Buddhists try to work on in their everyday lives by consciously remembering to give rather than take whenever they have the opportunity. This need not just mean being generous with money or material things. Some people have very little of material value to give, but still manage to be very generous – with their time, their energy, or with the non-material help, guidance, and support they give to others. Even to make the effort to stay sane, calm, and happy among people who have less control over their minds and feelings can be a very valuable act of giving. And often these non-material forms of generosity have a far greater impact on the world than any gift of goods or money.

Buddhists consciously try to express their generosity as a spiritual practice, but this is not seen as a painful duty – if giving feels painful this means that there is no real feeling of generosity behind it, and indicates that we need to look more closely at our motivations. As with all Buddhist ethics it is the attitude which is important, and although a generous attitude needs to be made real by action, the right action performed with the wrong attitude has little value.

In its negative sense, not taking the not-given means much more than not stealing. It implies that we should not manipulate others to get what we want in any way whatsoever – by playing on their greeds or fears, by using their guilt or pity to back them into corners, by wielding our power or authority, by exploiting their weakness, or just by outwitting them. And in the same way that we can give many things that have no material value, we can also take the not-given by making unwanted demands on people's time, energy, or emotions. Often these less direct forms of taking the not-given can be far more damaging than simple material theft. At a wider level this precept implies that we should take responsibility for our actions as consumers, investors, workers, or decision makers, and not lend our weight to activities that harm other people, animals, or the planet on which we live.

TO REFRAIN FROM SEXUAL MISCONDUCT

Buddhism does not see sex in itself as 'bad' – sexual repression can be a far greater evil – and it does not take moralistic stands against particular forms of sexual activity, such as masturbation, homosexuality, or sex 'out of wedlock'. However Buddhism does encourage us to liberate ourselves from all forms of slavery – including slavery to desires over which we think we have no control.

The positive principle behind this precept is that we should try to cultivate a wholesome contentment. One of the main enemies of contentment is craving, and for many people sexual desire is the strongest craving of all. The satisfaction of our sexual desires usually involves other people, and can have a major impact on our own lives and the lives of others. For these reasons sex is singled out in this precept. But to achieve contentment we need to get beyond our slavery to *all* forms of craving, and for some people the main enemy may be not sex but desire for food, drink, tobacco, excitement, high-tech gadgetry, power, recognition, achievement, a bigger house, or a faster car.

As long as we give in to craving for any of these things we put ourselves on a treadmill. We see the carrot dangling in front of our face, but somehow no matter how fast we move our legs we never seem to catch it. As soon as one want is satisfied another comes up to take its place, then another and another. We run faster and faster, always thinking that with the next sprint we will finally catch the carrot, and be able to sit down and enjoy our happiness in peace. But really things are not like that. Happiness does not come from catching the carrot – it cannot be caught. Happiness is there all the time for the taking if we would only stop running. Happiness never comes from satisfying our craving – craving is a state of mind that just grows stronger if we give in to it. Happiness comes from getting off the treadmill altogether, from seeing our craving for what it is and refusing to allow it to disturb our mind. Only then can we achieve the peace of mind we need to see things clearly, and only then will we have the energy left over to aim at higher things. This does not mean that we cannot enjoy sex, food, or anything else. It simply means that our minds and lives should not be ruled by our desire for these things.

Traditionally the negative form of this precept was interpreted to mean that the lay Buddhist should abstain from adultery, rape, and abduction. Obviously this interpretation needs some refinement if it is to give us any real guidelines for our sexual behaviour in modern society. All Buddhist ethical principles can be seen as elaborations of the first precept – not to cause harm to other living beings, including oneself – and this is no exception. Seen in this light, to refrain from sexual misconduct means that we should control our sexual desires so that they do not harm either ourselves or other people.

Our sexual desires harm us if we allow them to stop us from achieving peace of mind, a point we have already discussed. They might also harm us if we allow them to lead us mindlessly into relationships or situations that will be damaging for our growth.

We can also cause a great deal of pain to other people if we selfishly gratify our sexual cravings without taking others' needs into account. Buddhists therefore try to see sexual partners as important individuals with their own wants, needs, and fears, and never descend to exploiting others as sex objects in however subtle a way. This might include, for example, not entering into unequal relationships where the partner is likely to have expectations we have no intention of fulfilling. Buddhists would also try to avoid causing pain to third parties for the sake of sexual gratification, for example by engaging in sexual activity with one member of a settled couple.

Although Buddhism does not see sex as 'evil', complete abstinence from sexual activity has traditionally been regarded as an important practice for monks, nuns, and other people seriously following the spiritual path. In the days before effective contraception this was no doubt partly for practical reasons – supporting and rearing children needs a lot of time and energy, leaving little left over for spiritual practice. But celibacy is also an important spiritual practice in itself. For many people sexual desire is *the* major craving, and to be able to live in such a way that the mind is not constantly disturbed by this biological urge can be an enormous step towards peace of mind. Abstinence also makes energy available for other purposes, especially for meditation. Celibacy is normally associated with the monastic lifestyle, but periods of voluntary abstinence from sexual activity can probably be of benefit to any serious Buddhist, whatever his or her chosen way of life. In many Eastern Buddhist countries it is quite normal for laypeople to adopt the monastic lifestyle for limited periods – perhaps of a year, perhaps more. Many Western Buddhists who are not normally celibate also voluntarily refrain from any sexual activity for specific periods, perhaps for just a few weeks while on a meditation retreat, perhaps for much longer.

TO REFRAIN FROM UNTRUTHFULNESS

This precept implies much more than simply not lying. It asks us to be courageously open and straightforward. It asks us to be ourselves without any sense of shame, rather than hiding behind our ideas of what we would like to be, or what others would like us to be. This sort of courageous honesty allows us to see and accept ourselves as we are, and to begin to work on ourselves accordingly. It allows us to become authentic and wholehearted – and without wholehearted effort we can make no spiritual progress. And it allows us to develop genuine friendships, one of the main joys of life as a human being.

Most of us find it hard to accept ourselves as we really are, and we spend much of our time hiding behind a mask. Maintaining this mask uses a great deal of our energy, it causes us anxiety when we think we may be found out, and it introduces an element of shyness and insecurity into our relationships with other people that robs them of much of their warmth. Perhaps most damaging of all, we spend so much time behind our masks that we actually begin to fool even ourselves, and so find it impossible to see ourselves as we really are.

Being so used to hiding behind our masks, at first it can seem frightening to try to communicate honestly with other people, especially where this might mean revealing weaknesses or failures. But although it requires courage,

Buddhists make a conscious effort to be completely open with each other. And once the effort is made the actual experience of straightforward communication is immensely liberating. When we no longer have anything to hide many of the tensions that normally cloud our mental landscape vanish into thin air. We find that far from rejecting us for our 'undesirable' qualities, people respect and like us for what we are. Our relationships take on a new depth and warmth, and our friendships blossom. This brings a feeling of genuine self-esteem, and allows us to accept ourselves with kindness, warts and all. And only when we admit to ourselves that we do *have* warts can we begin to do anything about them.

Our attempts to keep some parts of ourselves hidden – even from ourselves – make us weak and flawed. These darker aspects of our personality do not go away because we refuse to acknowledge them. Instead they hide in the shadows and engage in guerrilla warfare within our psyche. We become divided within ourselves, so that our firmest resolutions get broken, our moods and priorities change from day to day, and even our best efforts are not fullhearted. To cure this fragmented condition we need to become more aware of our real feelings and motivations – a point we will return to when we discuss the next precept – and to do this we need to be honest both with others and with ourselves. As we learn to acknowledge and work on the less flattering aspects of our personality, the divisions within us gradually heal, and we become more authentic and solid, more capable of being wholehearted about our efforts to grow. We may even find that many of the parts of ourselves we hid so carefully turn out not to be undesirable at all, but – once accepted and skilfully used – turn into sources of great power and energy in our lives.

We have said before that each of the five precepts should be interpreted in the light of the first, and this is no exception – sometimes honesty needs to be tempered by goodwill. The fact that we honestly want to strangle our boss with his own tie does not mean that we should go ahead and do so in the interests of openness. And although some people may need to learn to lose their temper as a stage in coming to terms with their real emotions, our aim should be to be straightforward without inflicting damage on our fellow beings. Strong emotions – even anger – can be expressed without physical or emotional violence. This requires self-control – but conscious self-control is not at all the same thing as fear-ridden inhibition.

Our honesty or lack of it does not only influence our own states of mind, it also determines the quality of our interactions with others. If we refuse to be ourselves we do not allow other people to befriend us. Few people will befriend a mask.

Buddhism places great emphasis on friendship, and especially on friendship between people who share a spiritual aspiration. It is very difficult to make progress without this sort of fellowship. We need the encouragement and inspiration we get from like-minded people. We also sometimes need their kind criticism. We need friendships as an environment in which we can open our hearts and develop and express our warm feelings. And all of this is denied to us if we cannot be open and honest.

This is an area where it is particularly helpful to be in regular contact with other well-intentioned people who share our ideals and value real communication. Some people in our society do not welcome honesty. Others may not have our best interests at heart, and with such folk it might actually be foolish to be too honest. We should not use these facts to rationalize our desire to hide behind our masks, and most of us could benefit from being much more honest in almost all our relationships. But the fact remains that our society sometimes makes it very difficult to be open. Friendship between Buddhists, on the other hand, should provide an environment in which straightforward communication is valued, where it will be two-way, and where it will be accompanied by genuine goodwill and concern.

TO REFRAIN FROM CLOUDING THE MIND WITH DRINK OR DRUGS

Spiritual development involves both emotional growth and increased awareness. The positive principle behind this precept is that Buddhists should try to be as aware as possible at all times and in all places. The negative formulation warns us to beware of anything which dulls our awareness – drink and drugs are good examples, but it should be remembered that modern society also offers us many other ways of avoiding contact with reality.

The quality of awareness Buddhists strive for is often called mindfulness. This is a calm, lucid, appreciative attention to what is going on here and now. It means actually being present in the moment-to-moment business of living our lives. This is something that needs to be practised, and although meditation has the effect of increasing mindfulness, this alone is not enough. We need to make a determined effort to bring mindfulness into our daily lives for it to have a real effect.

Mindfulness has several dimensions. Firstly it involves being aware of ourselves – of our bodies, our thoughts, and our feelings. It involves paying attention to our surroundings. It involves being aware of other people as human beings rather than as cardboard cut-outs. And it involves trying to be aware of reality, or at least of bearing in mind such simple truths as that life is short, and that being a consumer may not be the most productive or noble use to make of it.

It takes a very real effort to develop mindfulness, both in meditation and – more to the point in discussing this precept – at all other times as well. But the effort is certainly worthwhile.

Firstly, mindfulness is very enjoyable. It brings an element of grace to even the simplest activities which makes them deeply pleasurable. It allows us to fully experience the beauty of the world and the joy of living in it. It cuts through hustle, bustle, and anxiety, and allows us to experience peace as an everyday reality.

Mindfulness also puts us in control. Unless we are aware, on a moment-to-moment basis, of our thoughts and moods and the feelings and motivations that drive them, we will have very little conscious control over the direction of our lives. Instead we are entirely at the mercy of our instinctive drives and subconscious urges. Only if we know clearly what is going on in our minds and hearts can we hope to behave as anything other than the victims of our past conditioning, and of our present external circumstances.

Lastly, mindfulness allows us to develop what could be described as true individuality. It provides a constant thread of awareness running through all the internal and external events we experience, giving us a sense of ourselves as developing beings with a future destiny. It allows us gradually to draw together all the many currents of our personality into one integrated whole. It helps us to become self-aware, self-motivated individuals, whose ideals and beliefs spring from inner richness and a clear-sighted view of the world, rather than from the opinions of other people around us.

If the positive principle behind this precept asks us to make the effort to maintain a degree of mindfulness under the difficult circumstances of modern life, the negative side asks us not to do anything that we know will make mindfulness more difficult. Drink and drugs are singled out because these were the main flights from reality available to people in the Buddha's time – and today they still serve the same purpose.

Buddhists do not take a sanctimonious attitude towards drinking – the point is that we should maintain our awareness, not that drink is evil – and most Buddhists in the West are not complete abstainers. But the fact remains that alcohol and other drugs *do* cloud the mind, and if we routinely use them to dull our awareness we will damage our progress. For this reason most Western Buddhists do not drink habitually, or to the point where their awareness becomes impaired. Many never drink at all. Most practising Buddhists find that as their normal state of mind becomes happier and their emotions warmer and more easily expressed, they simply lose the need to dismantle their inhibitions by drinking. Alcohol may be of temporary benefit to some people – particularly those who are very repressed – but Buddhists on the whole do not need to be drunk to be merry.

Since the Buddha's day human beings have ingeniously developed many other ways of avoiding contact with reality. Most of these go under the heading of entertainment (as opposed to genuine art). Mindless television, tabloid newspapers, computer games, pulp novels, even work – we can use all of these to distract ourselves from our experience of ourselves and the world around us. As with drink and drugs, this does not mean that occasionally watching soap operas or reading romantic novels is 'wrong'. But we should recognize that if we fill too much of our time with such distractions we will stunt our awareness and stop our growth.

These then are the five ethical principles that all practising Buddhists adopt: to try to be as kind, as generous, as contented, as honest, and as aware as possible, at all times and in all circumstances. If put into practice these principles can have a major effect on our lives and our states of mind, helping us to become clear, whole, and emotionally healthy. But however worthy these qualities may be, and however beneficial and far-reaching their effects, the five precepts are not ends in themselves. The practice of ethics is only the first of the three aspects of the threefold path of ethics, meditation, and wisdom.

An ethical life is the essential accompaniment to the practice of meditation. If we are to make real progress our meditation practice cannot be shut off from the rest of our life. Our meditation must be allowed to affect our life, and our life must reinforce our meditation. Without an ethical lifestyle – in the Buddhist sense – meditation cannot be fully effective, and the effects of meditation cannot spill over into our everyday state of mind.

Refrain From
1) Causing harm,
2) Taking what is not given
3) Sexual misconduct
4) Untruthfulness
5) Drink/Drugs- clouding mind

Kind
generosity
contentment
honest
aware

Four

MEDITATION

IF THE ETHICAL basis of our lives might be said to affect our minds indirectly, then meditation – the second aspect of the Buddhist path – is a way of exerting a more direct influence on our mental states. Meditation gives us a way of working on the mind *with the mind*, allowing us first of all to increase our overall awareness and positivity, and then to use this strengthened and purified awareness to see into the nature of things as they really are.

Although meditation is now almost a household word in the West, for most people it is still an unfamiliar concept, and it is not surprising that there are a number of very common misconceptions about what it really is. These include: that it is mainly a form of relaxation; that it is a trance state, a blissful flight from reality; that it is a form of self-hypnosis; and that it consists of making the mind blank. Certainly meditation *is* a powerful antidote to tension, and it *can* be blissful, but these benefits are by-products and not its main purpose. Meditation is not a trance, or a hypnotic or blank state of mind. It is a state of increased awareness in which we raise our level of being to new heights, not a way of reducing it to a semi-conscious haze.

Another common mistake about the nature of meditation is to identify it with one particular technique. A respected translator of Buddhist texts has said that there are over four hundred different techniques of Buddhist meditation. Obviously to equate any one of these techniques with meditation as a whole is to take far too narrow a view. Meditation is essentially a state of being, or rather a number of related states of being, and no one way of achieving it or working with it is 'correct' – although some may be more effective for certain people, or more appropriate for certain stages of our development.

All of the four hundred or so techniques of Buddhist meditation fall into two major categories, according to their purpose. These are 'samatha' techniques – the Pali word means, roughly, 'peace' or 'tranquillity' – and 'vipassana' or 'insight' techniques; some techniques have elements of samatha and vipassana.

SAMATHA MEDITATION

Samatha meditation calms the mind and focuses the awareness. It encourages positive emotion, and it expands our perspectives. This form of meditation is the essential preparation for the vipassana techniques – without this grounding the insight which vipassana meditation aims to encourage is very unlikely to arise. Our normal state of mind is too unconcentrated and divided, too clouded by negative emotion, too limited in its point of view to see reality as it really is.

Our normal level of awareness could be compared to a bad flashlight with a diffuse beam and flat batteries. It does not do much to lighten our darkness. The job of samatha meditation is to focus the beam and recharge the batteries, so that we can begin to see clearly. Or, to use a more traditional analogy, our normal state of mind could be likened to turbulent, muddy water, too clouded by swirling dirt for any light to pass through. Samatha meditation calms the turbulence of the mind and allows the mud to settle, so that the water becomes clear, bright, and lucid.

Most techniques of samatha meditation involve the use of a concentration object. This might be the process of breathing, a coloured disk, a candle flame, a mantra, or a positive emotion such as loving-kindness. Of these the breath is probably the most commonly used focus for the attention. This practice – often called 'mindfulness of breathing' – is described in detail by the Buddha in the early Buddhist writings, and it is used in one form or another by almost all Buddhist schools. Another common samatha practice is the 'development of loving-kindness', in which the meditator generates a strong feeling of loving-kindness towards both him- or herself and other people, in effect using this feeling as a meditation object.

These two meditation techniques give us a direct way of working on ourselves to cultivate two qualities which are central to spiritual development – awareness and warm-heartedness.

The mindfulness of breathing allows us to develop a level of concentrated mindfulness very rarely experienced in our normal life – for many people it comes as something of a revelation that it is possible to *be* so aware. If we are making an effort to maintain awareness as part of our practice of ethics, with time the mindfulness we develop in meditation will begin to seep into our everyday state of mind, giving us more clarity, more space in our life, and a new freedom to act creatively.

The 'development of loving-kindness' practice gives us a way of working directly on our emotions to increase our feelings of self-worth and our warm-heartedness towards others. Again, many newcomers to this practice are surprised that it is *possible* to feel such intense and warm emotion. And again, if the effects of the meditation are reinforced by our ethical practice, these feelings quite quickly begin to spill over into our everyday life, where they can seem to have an almost magical effect on our relationships with other people, and through these on our life in general.

All samatha techniques aim to induce a state of 'one-pointedness' in which the various parts of our being become united into a single, calm, bright awareness. If we are living an ethical life in conditions that encourage contentment and positive emotion, as we meditate the mental chatter that usually goes on in our heads soon gives way to a highly enjoyable feeling of light, quiet poise. Our internal conflicts begin to dissolve, and the neurotic and self-obsessed elements in our thinking are replaced by a wider and more objective point of view. Moving deeper into the meditative state we may experience surges of love and joy that seem to well up from our depths – in some people these may be strong enough literally to send shivers down the spine and stand the hair on end. Warm emotions come to saturate our being, so that our heart and mind become fused into a single faculty that views everything in a new and much brighter light. More experienced or gifted meditators may move even deeper, into completely engulfing states of inspiration in which the normal boundary between the self and the rest of the world begins to dissolve. Even so-called 'supernatural' powers may arise, such as the ability to exert a benevolent effect on other people's state of mind.

No doubt this sounds very exalted. But of course meditation is not always like this. Most people also have times when meditation means wrestling with a mind that is full of desire, anger, or conflict. At these times it can be hard work. But, even when the going is tough, meditation is useful work, because it allows us gradually to take control of these harmful states of mind, both in the meditation session and in the rest of our lives as well.

Although samatha meditation is a preparation for vipassana (or insight) practice, it should be obvious from what has been said that it is not just a boring preliminary – not something we have to get out of the way as soon as possible so that we can get on to 'the real thing'. If vipassana meditation did not exist, samatha meditation would still be very well worth the effort. Even when it is most difficult it gives us more leverage over our states of mind, and leaves us feeling calmer, more centred, and more positive. At its best it is profoundly enjoyable and can have far-reaching effects, giving our whole experience of life a clearer, brighter, and more expansive look.

VIPASSANA MEDITATION

For many people the most obvious effects of Buddhist practice are greater calm, warmth, positivity, and awareness, along with a growing sense of wholeness and contentment. But desirable as these qualities are, they are not treated as ends in themselves. These qualities are desirable, but they are not permanent. Even the healthiest human being can be affected by change. To make progress which will not be affected by circumstances – to rise above hardship, sickness, even old age and death – we need to become something more than a healthy human being. Mental health is a worthy goal, as far as it goes. But, beyond a certain point, insight – transcendental insight into the true nature of reality – is the cutting edge of spiritual growth.

Vipassana meditation practices are the techniques Buddhists use to encourage this insight. There are a very large number of these practices – probably most of the four hundred or so meditation techniques in the Buddhist tradition fall into this category. It would not be very useful to describe any of these practices in detail in a short book like this, but most do have some features in common.

The essential prelude to all vipassana techniques is to establish a deep and firm meditative state, by using a samatha practice like one of those we have already described. Once in this meditative state, the meditator might then allow their attention to rest on a symbolic representation of some aspect of ultimate reality – this might be a statement in words, or it might be a visual image. This symbolic representation is then allowed to permeate the meditator's heightened and purified awareness, so that it begins to trigger genuine insight into the truth which it represents. Alternatively, once in a firm meditative state, the meditator might concentrate on the nature of mind itself, or might become intensely aware of their whole moment-to-moment experience, with the aim of achieving direct insight into the nature of the reality being experienced.

We have already said that the sort of insight referred to by Buddhists does not just mean an intellectual understanding. This point cannot be emphasized enough. Our rational mind is only a small part of our psyche. A merely intellectual understanding of some point about the world or ourselves may come as a revelation, but it does little really to change our behaviour or modify our outlook. Genuine insight permeates – and alters – our whole being. To experience true insight we need to be in a special, higher state of being. This is why we need a firm foundation of ethics and samatha meditation before insight meditation will be effective. And this is why we cannot become enlightened by reading books, by studying, or by philosophizing – worthy as these activities may be in their place.

The ultimate aim of vipassana meditation is to allow insight to accumulate and mature to the point where it causes what has been called 'a turning about in the deepest seat of consciousness'. Once this happens there is no going back: such a deep and fundamental change has happened that there is no possibility of returning to older, narrower, and more selfish perspectives. From this point on, our whole being is flowing towards Enlightenment, and the only way we can go is forward.

Five

WISDOM

WISDOM, IN THE SENSE of the highest transcendental wisdom, is really the ultimate goal of the Buddhist path, rather than a step along the way. Wisdom in this sense is the same as Enlightenment – and like Enlightenment it cannot be expressed in words.

But at a lower level there are practical steps we can take to encourage the growth of wisdom, at least in its more mundane aspect. For one thing we can try to be more consistently mindful of those things that we *do* know, intellectually, to be true. For example we may know that if we give way to negative emotions such as hatred or craving we will feel unhappy. We may also know that our bodies are very small and short-lived phenomena in a very large universe. Most of us know both of these facts at an intellectual level. But very few of us actually behave as if we had ever heard of them. These and many other obvious realities seem to slip through our minds like water through a sieve. If we make an attempt to become more enduringly conscious of such facts we may at least change the way we *act* for the better, and in the longer term we will increase our objectivity and widen our perspective. Until we experience true insight this may be as close as we can get to developing wisdom.

Another way in which we can develop this lower level of wisdom is to study, understand, and bear in mind the verbal statements about the nature of reality made by people who are more developed than ourselves, and particularly by Enlightened beings. This alone will not give us insight, but again it will affect our behaviour and patterns of thought in a way that will accelerate our progress. And, as our practice of ethics and meditation ripens, this intellectual awareness may provide the basis for the growth of true insight.

Unfortunately in a short book we have little space to survey Buddhist philosophy, but in the next sections we will give a brief glimpse of two of the Buddha's most important statements about the human condition, the 'Three Characteristics of Conditioned Existence' and the 'Four Noble Truths'.

THE THREE CHARACTERISTICS OF CONDITIONED EXISTENCE

Insight into the conditioned nature of all phenomena is a central feature of Enlightenment. The Enlightened mind does not see the world as a collection of discrete 'things'. It perceives it as an endless web of cause and effect in which phenomena arise and disappear because the conditions exist for them to do so. Of course we too are part of this network of conditionality, and our birth and death, our thoughts, emotions, and actions are conditioned by events within and around us.

At first glance this might seem a fatalistic view, if it were not for the fact that Buddhism also offers us a vision of something above this state of bondage to circumstances.

This is the Unconditioned, or Buddhahood itself. But in order to move towards the Unconditioned we must first want to do so. And this involves taking a clear-sighted look at conditioned existence – the material world and our normal way of living within it – to see it for what it really is. Our vision of conditioned existence is usually highly coloured by wishful thinking. An understanding of the Three Characteristics of Conditioned Existence helps us to take off our rose-coloured glasses, and so to begin to think and act in a way that is appropriate to our real circumstances.

The Three Characteristics of Conditioned Existence are:
(1) that it is impermanent;
(2) that it is unsatisfactory; and
(3) that it is devoid of any unchanging, inherent self-nature.

Conditioned Existence is Impermanent

Everything in the universe is impermanent, nothing lasts, nothing is fixed, because the universe is by its very nature not a collection of stable entities, but a process of change. Our bodies, the houses we live in, the earth under our feet, and the mountains on the skyline are all in a constant state of flux. Some things change more quickly than others, but in the end everything that arises also eventually declines, dissolves, and becomes part of other phenomena.

In a few years, a few decades, or a few centuries – a mere blink of the eye in terms of the history of our planet – everything that now seems so important to us will have ceased to exist and become part of something else.

Most of us recognize this impermanence at an intellectual level. But we still become upset when one of our possessions breaks, when a relationship ends, or when we notice that we are growing older. We act – and in our heart of hearts we think – as though all things were unchangeable and permanent. And the tension created by trying to maintain an attitude which is so profoundly at odds with reality introduces a jarring and irritating quality into our everyday experience, because the real world is constantly slapping us in the face whenever it fails to match up to our illusions.

Conditioned Existence is Unsatisfactory

This statement, along with the first Noble Truth which will be discussed shortly, is often misinterpreted to mean that Buddhists believe that all life is suffering, and that – no matter how happy actual Buddhists seem to appear – Buddhism is a dour and pessimistic tradition. But of course the fact that conditioned existence is unsatisfactory does not mean that ordinary life is never enjoyable. What it does mean is that the material world and life as it is normally lived can never offer us complete and permanent satisfaction, for three reasons.

Firstly, life contains an inescapable element of actual suffering. No matter how hard we try to ignore the fact, at the very least we will all suffer illness, old age, and death. And unless we are very lucky we will also suffer our share of mental and physical pain on the way to this inevitable end. Secondly, conditioned existence is unsatisfactory because even those aspects of it which we enjoy are transient. Everything is impermanent, and what we cherish is bound to be taken away from us, so that even our pleasures will cause us suffering in the end, and our knowledge of this fact means that our present enjoyment is always tinged with sadness and anxiety. Thirdly, conditioned existence is unsatisfactory because something within us dimly perceives the existence of something higher, so that we will never be truly satisfied by our normal mundane life. Essentially we are square pegs in round holes, and until we rise above our habitual way of seeing ourselves and our lives we will experience the existential discomfort that comes from trying to fit into a situation which does not suit us.

An important implication of the inherently unsatisfactory nature of conditioned existence is that happiness is to be found not by changing the world around us to order it to our satisfaction, but by changing ourselves. This runs exactly counter to the accepted viewpoint within our society, which is that if only we could lay our hands on the right job, the right house, the right possessions, and the right relationship all would be well and we would live happily ever after. Of course we would not: even if we managed to obtain all these things we would soon want more, we would still yearn for something higher, and we would still suffer anxiety at the thought that we might lose what we had put so much effort into gathering around us. And in the end of course we *would* lose it all, because, as we have already seen, all conditioned things are impermanent.

Conditioned Existence is Devoid of any Unchanging, Inherent Self-Nature

This third characteristic of conditioned existence – that conditioned phenomena have no unchanging and inherent self-nature – is probably the most difficult of the three to grasp. For the practical purpose of our own personal development it is probably most important to concentrate on understanding one particular aspect of this feature of reality – the fact that our *own* self-nature is not fixed and permanent.

Most of us take the view that we have a fixed nature which is largely determined during our so-called formative years, or which is in some mysterious way essential to us, like a soul. We have certain likes, dislikes, opinions, habits, and emotional attitudes. We have certain weaknesses and certain strengths. And we feel that we can do very little to change what fate has made of us. This fixed view of ourselves is like a ball and chain which stops us escaping from the prison of our conditioning. It condemns us to a life of spiritual stagnation. But the reality is that, like everything else in the universe, our personality is impermanent, and this very impermanence should be seen as something highly positive. Each of us is a constantly changing process, and there is not one single aspect of ourselves that we cannot dramatically change for the better.

This view of ourselves and of the universe in general as a dynamic process rather than a collection of static 'things' is also perhaps the key to a wider understanding of the lack of any inherent self-nature in phenomena. The universe is a flux, a network of interacting conditions, but in order to make sense of it with our limited minds we quite artificially divide it up into discrete entities, giving each of these entities a name. This is a useful way of describing the universe for practical purposes, as long as we recognize its limitations. But we are so taken in by this picture that we imagine that the 'things' we name somehow exist independently of the universe around them, and of the conditions which keep them in existence – a mistaken view of the world and our part in it which causes us much suffering. In reality all conditioned phenomena – all the 'things' and beings in the universe, including ourselves – exist only as part of the wider whole, in the same way that an eddy in a stream only exists as part of the water around it. For this reason they cannot be said to have any real, inherent self-nature.

THE FOUR NOBLE TRUTHS

The Four Noble Truths are one of the best known and most important statements of Buddhist teaching – and one of the most widely misunderstood. These Four Truths – which the Buddha set out in his first major pronouncement after his Enlightenment, in about 528BCE – are as follows.

(1) The truth of the existence of suffering;

(2) the truth of the cause of suffering, which is egotistical desire and craving;

(3) the truth of the cessation of suffering, which is the cessation of egotistical desire; and

(4) the truth of the way to the cessation of suffering, which is the Noble Eightfold Path.

The word 'suffering' in these Truths is the usual, but rather extreme, English translation for an ancient Indian word *dukkha*, which can mean anything from actual physical pain to a sense of emptiness and dissatisfaction. This is exactly the same word which is translated as 'unsatisfactory' in discussing the characteristics of conditioned existence – so perhaps the first Noble Truth should really be called the 'truth of the existence of "unsatisfactoriness"'.

Like the second characteristic of conditioned existence – that life as normally lived is unsatisfactory – this Truth is often wrongly taken to imply that Buddhists believe that all life is suffering. They do not. But they do accept that suffering (or at least 'unsatisfactoriness') is a part – an integral part – of life as it is normally lived. This is not to be pessimistic, it is simply to be realistic. To pretend otherwise is not to be optimistic, it is to be profoundly deluded. This acceptance of the existence of suffering is the essential first step in trying to analyse the cause of the suffering and dissatisfaction in our lives, so that we can begin to find a cure – which is precisely what the remaining three Noble Truths proceed to do.

The second Noble Truth, that it is selfish desire which causes suffering, is the exact opposite of our normal point of view. We have been brought up to think that we become happy by satisfying our egotistical desires, by grabbing for ourselves the things we want. But in a world of constant change in which nothing is fixed or permanent, our desires are bound to be thwarted at every turn. And as long as we cling to these desires we are bound to experience dissatisfaction and suffering. It is precisely our egotistical desire which makes us unhappy, and the way to become happier is not to pander to our selfishness but to rise above it. This is not so much to destroy the self as to expand its limits; and the experience is not one of loss, it is one of release, joy, and love. The complete extinction of egotistical desire, which the third Noble Truth shows to be the way to the complete eradication of suffering, is equivalent to the complete self-transcendence of Buddhahood.

THE NOBLE EIGHTFOLD PATH

The fourth Noble Truth states that the way to achieve self-transcendence, and therefore the end of all suffering, is the Noble Eightfold Path. This consists of:

(1) Perfect vision (sometimes translated 'understanding')
(2) Perfect emotion (sometimes translated 'resolve')
(3) Perfect speech
(4) Perfect action
(5) Perfect livelihood

(6) Perfect effort

(7) Perfect awareness

(8) Perfect samadhi (sometimes translated 'concentration')

We are not going to explain the eight branches of this path in any detail, as this would involve going over much of the ground we have already covered, both in this chapter and under the headings of Ethics and Meditation. However we will say a few, more general, words about this particular formulation of the Buddhist path.

Perfect vision, which is often translated as right understanding, is placed at the head of this list in recognition of the fact that we need *some* perception that something greater and more satisfying lies beyond our normal experience before we will even begin to tread a spiritual path. At first this may be just a dim intuition or a merely intellectual understanding. But as we develop the other branches of the path this initial glimmer will intensify until it becomes the bright light of perfect vision in its fullest sense – so that this branch might be seen as both the first and last stage of the Path.

The remaining seven branches are sometimes called the 'Path of Transformation', as they represent the means by which we transform our whole being in the light of our vision of the truth. Perfect emotion, speech, action, livelihood, even effort and awareness could all be said to correspond to ethics in the very widest sense. Between them these branches cover every aspect of our lives, emphasizing the fact that Buddhist ethics is not a matter of following a set of rules, but involves the organization of our whole existence so that we cultivate higher states of consciousness. Effort and awareness are both also clearly involved in the practice of meditation, along with the last branch of the Eightfold

Path, perfect samadhi. The word 'samadhi' has been left untranslated because no satisfactory English equivalent exists. 'Samadhi' is sometimes used to mean merely concentration, sometimes to mean meditation, and sometimes to mean a profound meditative state which is equivalent to the subjective experience of Enlightenment. Used here, as the last branch of the Eightfold Path, it is clear that samadhi certainly does not mean just concentration, nor even just meditation in the normal sense, but also the fruits of meditation and of the whole path – the experience of Buddhahood itself.

Six

DEVOTIONAL PRACTICE

BUDDHISM HAS NO omnipotent creator god. This is an attractive feature of the tradition for many people, so that it can come as a surprise – and not necessarily a welcome one – to discover that Buddhists take part in practices that look, on the surface at least, very much like religious worship. What is the role of devotional practice in a tradition with no creator god? And what have images of the Buddha, bowing, chanting, and ritual got to do with becoming a more aware, emotionally positive human being?

Devotional practice in Buddhism might mean something as simple and unstructured as gazing at a statue of the Buddha, and perhaps experiencing a sense of quiet peace. It might mean chanting a few traditional verses. It might mean conjuring up a colourful mental visualization. Or it might mean taking part in a dramatic and moving ritual with other people, perhaps incorporating poetry, music, readings, incense, and offerings.

But whatever the form such practices take, their main purpose is always the same – to nurture and strengthen our devotion. This means both devotion in the sense of commitment to making real progress along the path, as well as devotion in the sense of a self-transcending attitude that sees the real importance of life as lying in something above and beyond our own small wants and fears. These two aspects – devotion as commitment on the one hand, and devotion as self-transcendence on the other – may well be inseparable, but for convenience we will look at them one at a time.

DEVOTION AS COMMITMENT

If we want to be successful in any field – in the arts, in scholarship, in sports, in any profession or craft – we need dedication and commitment. We need devotion. There can be no real achievement without struggle, and there can be no struggle without the commitment that keeps us going when it would be easier to give up. Even to achieve some quite ordinary aim, like success in business, takes long hours of hard work, gritty determination, and a willingness to sacrifice other pleasures and opportunities. In other words it takes real devotion to a goal, as well as dedication to doing whatever is necessary to reach it. Spiritual achievement is certainly no easier than achievement in business, and it is not surprising that to make any real spiritual progress we also need a strong devotion to our goal, as well as a firm dedication to the tools that help us reach it.

The ultimate ideal for all Buddhists – the goal – is of course Enlightenment, personified by the Buddha. The tools that help us move towards Enlightenment are the Buddhist teachings, called 'Dharma' in Sanskrit, along with the spiritual community of committed Buddhists, who can teach, encourage, and support us – the 'Sangha'. These three – the Buddha, the teachings, and the community – are the main

Buddha   Dharma   Sangha

objects of devotion in all schools of Buddhism, and are often known as the 'Three Jewels'. When somebody firmly commits themselves to these three they are said to 'go for refuge'. It is this 'going for refuge' that makes somebody a Buddhist.

The phrase 'going for refuge' can be an obstacle for some people when they first come across it, as it can seem – quite wrongly – to imply hiding or running away. But when we think about the meaning of the phrase we should remember that it is not only Buddhists who go for refuge – everybody goes for refuge to *something*. We go for refuge to whatever we put at the centre of our lives. Often we go for refuge to different things at different times. We can go for refuge to physical pleasures like food or sex. We can go for refuge to money, comfort, career, or security; to some subcultural style; or to drink; or to a drug. We can go for refuge to our sexual partner, to our family, or to our friends. To go for refuge to the Buddha, the Buddhist teachings, and the spiritual community, means that there has been a fundamental shift in our priorities so that such unreliable and – in the end – unsatisfying refuges no longer sit at the centre of our life. Instead we have begun to see that our real well-being depends on our spiritual progress, and have begun to develop the commitment we need to make this vision an effective force in our lives.

Perhaps it is easy to see that we need commitment if we are to get anywhere with our practice of Buddhism. But why do we need devotional *practices* – which when we first come across them can seem strange, alien, and even embarrassing?

To set ourselves free from our conditioning we need to break out of old, deeply ingrained ways of acting, thinking, and feeling. Anyone who has tried to change even one or two of their own old patterns knows that it is not easy. Just seeing that the change makes sense is not enough to make it happen. To have the strength and the consistency of purpose to shift old patterns we need to be genuinely inspired. We also need to be reminded – often – of our determination to change, so that we can fight off the constant, downward pull of our old habits. These are two of the main purposes of devotional practices – to inspire, and to remind.

One way of getting an idea of how devotional practice can help us in this way is to imagine what it would be like if, instead of living at the present time and being surrounded by our present friends, we lived instead with the Buddha and his followers, some 2,500 years ago. It is easy to imagine that if we had regular daily contact with the Buddha, constantly hearing him teach, mingling with his highly developed followers, it would have a dramatic effect on us. If we had, right now, sitting in front of us, talking to us, a being of clear, expansive wisdom, of complete openheartedness, and of limitless energy, the effect would be electric. We would be shocked out of our rut. We would be inspired. And our own growth towards Enlightenment would be given a sudden, powerful boost.

If we had such a being sitting in front of us not just once, not just today, but every day, this effect – this eye-opening shock – would be multiplied over and over. We would be constantly inspired, and constantly reminded of what is important, as well as of what is not. Our lives would be changed radically, and we would suffer none of the inertia, doubt, distraction, and conflict between different goals that we normally experience. Instead our energies would become strong, unified, and powerfully directed towards the goal of Enlightenment – and with such energies we would literally work wonders.

Unfortunately we do not live with the Buddha. And even if we have a teacher who might serve – at least in part – as a proxy for the Buddha, we are unlikely to see them very often. But if we cannot be in the daily physical presence of an Enlightened being, we can put ourselves in frequent, even daily, contact with the Buddha *in our imagination*, through some form of devotional practice. And this regular imaginative contact can have many of the same effects. It can inspire us – especially if we give our imagination and emotions free rein. And at a more down-to-earth level it can constantly remind us of the important things in our life, keeping us in touch with our spiritual frame of reference, concentrating our energies, and preventing us from being undermined by the barrage of unhelpful conditioning the world throws at us.

DEVOTION AS SELF-TRANSCENDENCE

To get anywhere with our practice of Buddhism we need to devote our energies to making this happen – this is an important fact, and an important reason for devotional practice. But it is not the only one. Another aspect of devotion is dedication to something higher and wider than our own little wants and fears. Devotion in this sense is an attitude to life that shifts our priorities, taking importance away from our small personal preoccupations, and giving it to broader, more important concerns. A devotional attitude in this sense might involve, for example, dedication to our teacher, or to making the Buddhist teachings more widely known, or to helping our friends in the spiritual community. Ultimately it might manifest as a fierce desire to do whatever we can to be of help to the universe, and particularly to help our fellow sentient beings.

Devotion in this sense is a feature of spiritual development. It is an aspect of our broadened vision, and a facet of our liberation from our usual obsession with ourselves. As we grow our devotion increases. As our devotion increases, we grow. For this reason devotional practice contributes directly to our progress towards Enlightenment. One of the ways it does this is by helping us discover and deepen certain powerful emotions – reverence, gratitude, celebration, a warm sense of our shared community with others, and a sense of the awesome beauty and mystery of existence. These emotions are part of our response to any moves we make towards self-transcendence. Their effect is to leave the walls we build around ourselves just that little bit thinner and more transparent. Over time, regular devotional practice – the regular experience of these expansive emotions – can gradually alter our whole approach to existence, so that instead of constantly asking what the world can do for us, we begin to grow out of our spiritual childhood, and ask what we can do for the world.

DEVOTION AND THE NEWCOMER

Devotional practice is a creative exercise of the imagination. It is not a gesture of faith in any dogma, a submission to any supernatural power, or a petition for favours from above. As with any mental exercise it gets easier the more we do it, but there is no reason why a newcomer to Buddhism should not take part in devotional practice without feeling that they are compromising themselves in any way. We do not have to believe that the characters in a book, a film, or a play are real in order to enter into it in our imagination – and perhaps have our emotions stimulated and refined in the process. In the same way we do not have to have any particular belief in the Buddha or anything else to take part in Buddhist practice. We can enter into it in just the same spirit that we might give ourselves to a work of fiction, simply suspending our natural – and often healthy – scepticism, at least for the duration of the 'performance'.

But although devotional practice is a creative exercise, it would be wrong to cynically dismiss it as 'just' imagination, and for that reason somehow unreal. When we 'imagine' ourselves in the presence of the Buddha, for example, we can contact real and powerful forces, forces that exist in their own right, and that can have strong positive effects on us and on our lives. This may be hard to accept for those who have never experienced it, but it is a fact. Part of the explanation is that, because we all have something of Buddhahood hidden inside us, devotional practice can put us in touch with unexplored potentials *within ourselves* – our own wisdom, our compassion, our nobility, our strength, our capacity for enlightened action, and our own inner teacher. By helping us uncover our own hidden riches in this way, Buddhist devotional practice can be a potent technique for bringing out our own neglected powers.

Seven

SOME HISTORY

BUDDHISM IS AN ANCIENT tradition, and in the course of its long history it has adapted to meet the needs of many different cultures, and also of some very different temperaments and types of human being. As a result it now flourishes in a number of apparently quite different forms, which can be confusing for the Westerner. In this chapter we will give a very brief outline of how Buddhism has developed over the last two and a half millennia, in the hope of clearing up some of this confusion.

THE EARLY BUDDHISTS AND THE ORIGIN OF THE MONASTIC LIFESTYLE

During the Buddha's lifetime and for many years after his death, his followers formed a loose-knit community of both what we might call 'full-timers' – men and women who devoted their entire energies to their spiritual development and to teaching and guiding others – and laypeople who combined these tasks with the more mundane business of earning a living and bringing up children. What united these people was simply that they had all 'gone for refuge'

– that is, committed themselves to striving towards Enlightenment, to putting the Buddha's teaching into practice, and to treating one another with friendliness, love, and compassion.

The full-timers among this 'sangha' – as the Buddhist community was and still is called – although they renounced all material possessions, were not nuns or monks in the usual sense. They did not live in monasteries, and for most of the year they walked from place to place, living in the open air and begging for their food, in much the same way as the Buddha had done in his lifetime. Only in the rainy monsoon season did they settle down, coming together in huts or shelters to meditate and study together. In time these rainy season retreats became larger and more formalized, and more and more monks and nuns stopped travelling and settled in them throughout the year. These retreats are the origin of the monastic tradition which has become such a major feature of some schools of Buddhism.

THERAVADA AND MAHAYANA

As the Buddhist community fanned out into different areas of India it quite quickly became divided into a number of different schools. But despite their differences in emphasis these remained on good terms with one another, and Buddhists from different schools would meet and communicate regularly, even living and practising under the same roof. This spirit of tolerance has been a continuing feature of Buddhism, and still largely exists today.

But by about the first century CE two major branches of the Buddhist tradition had developed: a more conservative branch – its detractors called it the Hinayana, or 'lesser way'

– and a more flexible branch known as the 'greater way', or Mahayana, by its champions.

Today the main representative of the more conservative trend is the Theravada School of South-east Asia – the name Theravada means 'way of the elders'. Theravadin Buddhists base their teachings on what is known as the Pali Canon, a collection of writings recorded in the Pali language of northern India during the first century BCE. By this time these teachings had already been passed down through an oral tradition for several hundred years, and been standardized, harmonized, and – no doubt – added to. But for all its inevitable inaccuracies and additions, the Pali Canon is still probably an accurate record of many of the Buddha's spoken teachings, possibly expressed in something very like the actual words he used. Followers of the 'Way of the Elders' place great emphasis on the historical authenticity of their teachings, and are loath to adopt any practices that are not specifically described in the Pali Canon. For this reason the Theravada represents a more conservative strand within the Buddhist tradition than the Mahayana, whose followers have always been more willing to adapt their teachings and practices to suit different circumstances and personalities.

MAHAYANA BUDDHISM AND THE BODHISATTVA IDEAL
Mahayana Buddhism seems to have arisen – at least in part – as a response to what some Buddhists saw as degenerations in the practices of existing schools. These appear to have included a literalistic emphasis on the Buddha's recorded words, sometimes at the expense of the spirit of his teaching; a tendency to see the monastic life as the only road to Enlightenment; and a tendency to see the quest for Enlightenment as a selfish search for personal liberation.

To counteract these trends Mahayana Buddhists made a deeper exploration of the philosophical implications of the Buddha's teachings and their own spiritual experience. They attempted to find or reinstate forms of practice which were suitable for the laypeople as well as those who lived a monastic life. And they re-emphasized the importance of cultivating a warm, compassionate attitude toward other living beings.

In keeping with this new emphasis, Mahayana Buddhism developed a much more explicit stress on selfless, compassionate action, and a new version of the Buddhist spiritual ideal, distinct from the older ideal of the 'Arhant' – roughly 'Worthy One' – which in the minds of some people had come to imply a lofty detachment from ordinary humanity. The spiritual ideal for Mahayana Buddhism is not simply a being who is liberated from the suffering of this world and lives in a state of bliss. It is someone who has seen beyond the world as we know it, but still chooses to work in the world and for the good of the world, out of a deep sense of compassion and unity with all living things.

This new ideal was called, in Sanskrit, the bodhisattva. The word bodhisattva means, literally, 'wisdom being', and it refers to someone whose whole energy is directed towards the attainment of Enlightenment – but for the sake of all beings, rather than for personal liberation. The bodhisattva ideal served a dual purpose for followers of the Mahayana. Firstly it stressed the selfless, compassionate aspect of Enlightenment which they felt some Buddhists had lost sight of. Secondly it offered a goal that could be aimed at by *all* Buddhists – whether or not they lived a monastic lifestyle – because it placed more emphasis on altruistic action in the world.

VAJRAYANA BUDDHISM — THE 'DIAMOND WAY'

From about 500CE a third major branch of Buddhism began to emerge in India. This was Tantric Buddhism, which became known as the Vajrayana, or 'diamond way'. The Vajrayana uses a range of powerful symbols and rites to contact and engage the full subconscious energies of the individual, and to use these energies to propel the practitioner towards Enlightenment. Tantric Buddhism is an 'esoteric' tradition, in the sense that it depends heavily on direct initiation or 'empowerment' by a guru, and that it can only be properly practised under the close guidance of a spiritual teacher. It is an advanced form, for those who have already developed strong self-control and a highly compassionate attitude. For others its methods would be useless or even dangerous, and for this reason Vajrayana teachers traditionally choose their disciples very carefully to ensure that their motives are selfless and pure, and that they can control the energies released by Tantric practice.

DECLINE AND EXPANSION

Between about 900 and 1100CE – by which time it had existed in India for about 1,500 years – Buddhism virtually died out in the land of its birth. The final cause of its disappearance was a series of invasions from the West, by Moslems who destroyed the Buddhist monasteries and universities and massacred many monks. But although the spread of Islam passed the death sentence on Buddhism in India, certain features of Indian Buddhism at this time contributed to its own decline. It had become centralized in huge monastic complexes which were vulnerable to destruction by force. It had become dependent on the support of rich and powerful benefactors. And it had lost touch with the ordinary people of the Indian village. Hinduism, which was deeply rooted in everyday village life, proved much better able to survive the hostility of the Moslems.

But long before Buddhism vanished from India it had already spread in all directions far beyond the limits of the Indian subcontinent. As early as the third century BCE it became the official religion of Sri Lanka, and from there it spread south and east into Thailand, Burma, and Cambodia, in the form of the Theravada School. Today the 'Way of the Elders' is still the main spiritual tradition of this area.

The later Mahayana branch spread into Central Asia, throughout the Himalayan region, and on into the vast empire of China, and from there into Mongolia, Korea, Japan, and Vietnam, becoming by far the largest branch of the tradition. The spread of the still later Vajrayana branch followed a similar path to the Mahayana, expanding into the Himalayas, Tibet, China, Mongolia, and Japan, although as an advanced and 'esoteric' form of the tradition it never achieved the same following as the Mahayana.

BUDDHISM IN THE WEST

The West first began to become aware of Buddhism as something other than a form of heathen idol-worship in the nineteenth century. Some of the many Westerners who visited the Buddhist East realized that the tradition had something valuable to offer, as shown for example by Sir Edwin Arnold's epic poem, 'The Light of Asia'. But most of those who wrote about Buddhism took a mainly scholarly interest in the subject. Scholars were attracted by the rational, analytical approach of the Theravada School of South-east Asia, and especially by the fact that the Theravada based its teachings on a collection of scriptures which are as close as we can get to the actual words of the Buddha. Such scholars – and particularly some influential British ones – tended to think of the Theravada as 'real' Buddhism, and to dismiss the Mahayana and Vajrayana as later corruptions – and corruptions which made too many concessions to the emotional aspects of human nature for their taste.

During the first half of the twentieth century, Theravadin Buddhism continued to be the best-known and most respected form of the tradition in the West, although information about other forms gradually trickled into the public awareness. In the last thirty or so years this trickle has become a flood, and several different schools have become fashionable at different times, notably the Japanese Zen form of the Mahayana, and rather more recently Tibetan Buddhism – a rich mixture of the Mahayana and Vajrayana traditions.

Much of this interest has been purely intellectual, and there are uncounted people in the West whose only involvement is through books. But there are also an ever-increasing number of practising Buddhists in Western countries, and Buddhist temples, monasteries, communities, public centres, and retreat centres have grown up all over Europe and North America. These represent a variety of traditional Eastern schools, as well as some newer groups such as the Friends of the Western Buddhist Order, an indigenous Western movement which is not linked to any one Eastern cultural form.

It seems that Buddhism has come to the West to stay – perhaps because it is so badly needed. As a society our most important problems are no longer material – we already have enough goods and enough mastery of the physical world, if only we would use them wisely. Today our problems are mainly mental, emotional, and spiritual. And although these problems have their roots in the hearts and minds of individual human beings, their effects are global. As a race we are now so powerful that if we do not deal with the greed, hatred, and fear that drive so much of our activity we are very likely to turn our beautiful planet into a wasteland, perhaps destroying ourselves in the process.

Those of us who already call ourselves Buddhists can be excused for thinking that the development of a widespread new spiritual perspective based on the gentle sanity of the Buddhist tradition may be one of the few ways in which such a catastrophe can be prevented. But even we would admit that to think of Buddhism as a solution to the world's problems – at least at the moment – is more than a little premature. Before we solve our planet's problems we need to pay attention to that small part of the planet for which we have a unique responsibility – ourselves, and our own relationships with other people and the world around us. And it is at this level – at the level of the individual human being and his or her life – that Buddhism can already be seen to have had a noticeable impact on the West. Even in the last few decades the ideas and practices which have been briefly described in this short book have had a deep effect on many people, giving them a new set of more worthwhile goals, a new warmth in their dealings with others, and a new and more joyful appreciation of what it means to be a human being.